Amelia Earhart

A Buddy Book
by
Christy DeVillier

ABDO
Publishing Company

VISIT US AT

www.abdopub.com

Published by ABDO Publishing Company, 4940 Viking Drive, Edina, Minnesota 55435.
Copyright © 2001 by Abdo Consulting Group, Inc. International copyrights reserved in all
countries. No part of this book may be reproduced in any form without written permission
from the publisher.

Printed in the United States.

Edited by: Michael P. Goecke
Contributing Editor: Matt Ray
Image Research: Deborah Coldiron, Susan Will
Graphic Design: Jane Halbert
Cover Photograph: Archive Photos
Interior Photographs/Illustrations: pages 11, 12, 14 & 25: Archive Photos; pages 5, 6, 7, 8,
10, 13, 16, 17, 19, 20, 21, 22, 23, 24 (right), 26 & 27: courtesy of Atchison County Historical
Society, Amelia Earhart Collection, Atchison, KS; page 15: Corbis; pages 24 (left) & 28:
Deborah Coldiron

Library of Congress Cataloging-in-Publication Data

Devillier, Christy, 1971-
    Amelia Earhart / Christy Devillier.
        p. cm. — (First biographies)
    Includes index.
    ISBN 1-57765-596-6
    1. Earhart, Amelia, 1897-1937—Juvenile literature. 2. Women air pilots—United
States—Biography—Juvenile literature. [1. Earhart, Amelia, 1897-1937. 2. Air pilots. 3.
Women—Biography.] I. Title. II. Series.

TL540.E3 .D477 2001
629.13'092—dc21
[B]
                                                                            2001022018

Table of Contents

Why Is She Famous?

Amelia Earhart was a skilled airplane pilot, or aviator. She set many records. Some of them are:

- First woman to fly alone across the Atlantic Ocean
- First person to fly alone from Hawaii to California
- First person to fly alone from California to Mexico
- First person to fly alone from Mexico to New Jersey

Amelia Earhart

Amelia Earhart is famous for believing in herself. In the 1930's, many people believed that women could not do certain things. Earhart showed that these people were wrong. Amelia showed the world that women can accomplish as much as men.

Amelia's Family

Amelia Earhart was born in Atchison, Kansas on July 24, 1897. The Earhart family moved a lot. Amelia lived in Kansas City (Kansas), Minnesota, Illinois, and Iowa.

Amelia was close to her family. Her mother was Amy Otis. Her father was Edwin. Amelia had a younger sister named Muriel.

Baby Amelia and her mother.

Amelia at age 10.

Amelia and Muriel were tomboys. They sometimes wore pants. Edwin took Amelia and Muriel fishing. The girls asked for a football for Christmas one year. Football was a boy's game. Yet, Amelia's parents did not mind giving a football to them.

Growing Up

Amelia (right) and
Muriel (left) with family.

There are many stories about Amelia as a child. Friends and family say she loved adventure. She enjoyed discovering new things to do. She was not often afraid of danger.

Amelia liked to read adventure stories, too. A favorite book of Amelia's was Black Beauty. Black Beauty is about a horse. Amelia and Muriel loved horses.

Amelia saw her first airplane when she was 11 years old. It was at the Iowa State Fair.

A Young Feminist

In the early 1900's, people expected girls and women to act in a certain way. There were rules for acting like a lady. Amelia did not pay much attention to these rules. Amelia Earhart was an early feminist.

Amelia Earhart was a feminist.

Amelia liked to wear pants.

Amelia loved many sports and games. She enjoyed tennis, bicycling, and basketball. She liked to play boy's games, too. She did not understand why girls could not play these games. Amelia wondered why the rules for boys and girls were different.

Amelia Earhart loved adventure.

First Steps

At 19, Amelia went to Ogontz School in Philadelphia, Pennsylvania. Two years later, she became a nurse's aide. She helped soldiers at Spadina Military Hospital. These soldiers were hurt in World War I.

Amelia studied at Ogontz School.

At Spadina, Amelia talked to these soldiers. They told her stories about flying. She liked these stories. So, Amelia visited the nearby airfield.

A World War I airplane pilot.

In Love With Flight

Amelia moved to California in 1920. There, she went to her first air show. Airplane pilots were doing tricks, or stunts. Amelia enjoyed the air show very much.

Wing-walking is one airplane stunt.

Later, Amelia decided to learn to fly.
Amelia's teacher was Anita Snook.
Anita was a woman pilot. Anita's
lessons cost a lot of money. So,
Amelia worked odd jobs to pay
for these lessons.

Amelia took flying lessons.

In 1922, Amelia's family helped her buy an airplane. The airplane was a Kinner Airster. This airplane was bright yellow.

Amelia called her first airplane the Canary.

Crossing The Atlantic

Amelia moved to Boston, Massachusetts in 1926. She worked with the Denison airport there. People started to find out that Amelia was a good pilot.

One day, Captain Hilton Railey asked Amelia to fly across the Atlantic Ocean. This was a dangerous flight. Many people had died trying to fly across the Atlantic. Yet, Amelia was brave. She said yes.

Amelia flew from Newfoundland to Wales on a plane called Friendship. She did not pilot the plane. Still, Amelia was the first woman to fly across the Atlantic. Amelia wrote a book about this flight.

Amelia wrote *20 Hours—40 Minutes.*

In 1929, Amelia helped to form a group of women pilots. They called themselves the Ninety-Nines. They asked Amelia to be their first president.

Amelia and a few of the Ninety-Nines.

Amelia And George

Amelia married George P. Putnam in 1931. George was a publisher. He had published books by Charles Lindbergh. Charles Lindbergh was a famous pilot. Some people said Amelia reminded them of Charles Lindberg. Sometimes, George called Amelia "Lady Lindy."

"Lady Lindy" and her husband, George Putnam.

Back then, a married woman took her husband's last name. This was another rule that Amelia did not follow. This early feminist kept Earhart as her last name.

George and Amelia were partners in marriage and in work. George published two of Amelia's books.

Amelia Earhart kept her last name.

Fame For Amelia

In 1932, Amelia flew a plane by herself across the Atlantic Ocean. She was the first woman to do this. This flight made Amelia very famous.

A crowd welcomes Amelia Earhart.

Amelia started to win everyone's attention. She won the National Geographic Society's Special Gold Medal. Another award came from the United States. It was the Distinguished Flying Cross. Amelia was the first woman to receive both of these awards.

The Distinguished Flying Cross

Amelia wearing the Distinguished Flying Cross.

Amelia Earhart and Eleanor Roosevelt.

President Franklin Roosevelt often asked Amelia and George to the White House. Amelia became a friend of the President's wife, Eleanor Roosevelt.

Fearless Spirit

  Back in the 1930's, it was not common to travel in airplanes. Also, it was not safe to fly long distances. Amelia understood the danger. She was afraid sometimes. Yet, she did not back down. Amelia went on to set more records.

America loved Amelia's fearless spirit.

Amelia's final flight around the world was very risky. She planned to fly along the equator. She wanted to circle the entire earth. Her spirit of adventure drove her forward.

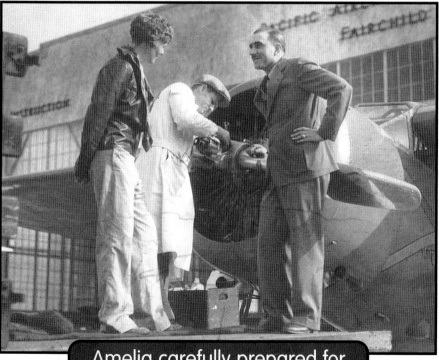

Amelia carefully prepared for her around-the-world flight.

Amelia's Greatest Feat

Amelia visited 19 countries on her last flight. She saw Venezuela, Brazil, Africa, India, Australia, and New Guinea.

Amelia finished two-thirds of her last flight. That's over 22,000 miles. Then, on July 3, 1937, she disappeared. Many people tried to find her. They found no clues.

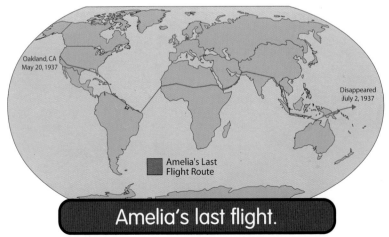

Oakland, CA
May 20, 1937

Disappeared
July 2, 1937

Amelia's Last
Flight Route

Amelia's last flight.

What happened to Amelia Earhart? Did she run out of fuel? Did she crash-land on an island? To this day, nobody is sure what happened to Amelia.

Amelia Earhart did not fly around the world. Yet, she is a very important person. She set many records as a pilot. Even greater, she showed the world that women are not just ladies. Women have talent and skill equal to men. Everyone can learn from Amelia's spirit of adventure.

Important Dates

July 24, 1897 Amelia Earhart is born.

1908 Amelia sees her first airplane.

1918 Amelia nurses World War I soldiers at Spadina Military Hospital.

1920 Amelia takes flying lessons from Anita Snook.

1922 Amelia buys her first airplane, the Canary.

1928 Amelia flies across the Atlantic Ocean. She is the first woman to do this.

1931 Amelia marries George P. Putnam.

1932 Amelia flies across the Atlantic Ocean by herself.

June 1, 1937 Amelia begins her flight around the world.

July 3, 1937 The last time anyone hears from Amelia Earhart.

Important Words

adventure going somewhere new or trying something new without being afraid of danger.

airfield a place for airplanes.

aviator a pilot, or a person who flies airplanes.

equator an imaginary circle that divides the earth into two equal parts.

feminist someone who believes men and women are equal.

fuel something that powers a machine like an airplane.

publisher someone who makes and sells books or magazines.

World War I the first war between many countries that happened from 1914-1918.

Web Sites

Amelia Earhart
http://www.ellensplace.net/eae_intr.html
The Amelia Earhart web site gives details on Amelia's early life, her celebrity years, and her last flight.

Amelia Earhart Museum
http://www.ameliaearhartmuseum.org/
This fact-filled site includes stories about Amelia's childhood and plenty of pictures.

Index